Star of Wonder

The story of the Wise Men
Matthew 2:1–11 and Luke 2:1–18, and
Numbers 24:17 and Revelation 22:16,
for children

Written by Cynthia A. Hinkle
Illustrated by Johanna van der Sterre

Long, long ago, Christmas had no snow;
Folks wore flowing robes and sandals.
In a land of spices, cinnamon, and rice,
People rode donkeys and camels.

But the folks, you see, were like you and me.
They were sinful, mean, and hurting.
Like us they sighed, like us they cried.
We all need God's love and forgiving.

So God had a plan that was bold and grand.
He would send us a loving Savior
To old Bethlehem. To point to Him,
God lit the bright Star of Wonder.

A state's decree counting folks 1-2-3
Brought Mary and Joseph to town.
In the small city, a place not pretty,
Love's perfect, sweet starlight came down.

Happy and weepy, Mary, quite sleepy,
Placed sweet Baby in a hay nest.
Jesus, the Newborn, was safe and warm.
Now, perhaps, Mom can rest.

Above the town, and all around
The hills whispered with desert grass.
Lambs nibbled, shepherds talked and giggled
And the stars sparkled as hours passed.

On Bethlehem fields, the shepherds kneeled,
Each shaking in wonder and fright.
Perfect and clear, bright, shiny, and near,
God's glory filled up the night.

There wasn't a doubt, an angel did shout,
"Do not be afraid! It's good news!
There's a new Baby Boy who brings great joy
For everyone, even for you!

"In King David's town, cloth wrapped around
In a manger your Savior lies."
To which angel throngs in the sky sang songs,
"Glory, glory to God on high!"

The angels took flight, still went the night
As the shepherds started to run.
"Off to Bethlehem. Let's race! Let's see Him!
Let's see what our Lord God has done!"

So guests came gawking, telling and talking
Of the Baby—an amazing story!
The skies afire as angel choirs
Sang, "He's the Savior, God's Glory!"

Mary wiped her eyes, their news no surprise;
An angel had already told her.
Son of God is He, mighty King He'll be,
On the throne He'll rule forever.

Months later, at home, how Jesus had grown!
He was crawling all over the floor.
He heard camels bray as He gurgled away
When some Wise Men came to the door.

From afar these men came and by the same
Star of wonder, caravanned to the west.
On the shifting sands, sky maps in hand,
Many miles they marched on their quest.

Then while Mary looked, to Jesus each took
Gifts of myrrh, frankincense, and gold;
For old, old rolls of written paper scrolls
To them the King's birth had foretold.

Born in a stall, Jesus Christ came so small,
The humble, yet great Lord and King.
He lived, died, then rose to save all from sins' woes.
We're forgiven, with life free and lasting!

Lord, help us tell, You are Emmanuel,
God with us, Christ Jesus, You are.
Through true stories, by grace Your glories
Shine for us, for all, like the star!

Dear Parents,

"And we have the word of the prophets made more certain, and you will do well to pay attention to it, as to a light shining in a dark place, until the day dawns and the morning star rises in your hearts." (1 Peter 1:19)

At last the Light had come! The shepherds looked to the sky, heeded the angels' announcement, and came to see. The Wise Men looked to the sky, followed the star, and came to worship. Even wicked Herod took the sign seriously and did what he could to lessen the impact of this new King.

At last the Light had come! After centuries of waiting, the prophecies of the Messiah were fulfilled. God's promised Savior had come, offering forgiveness, peace, and boundless hope to the sin-darkened world. *"Jesus spoke to them, saying, 'I am the light of the world. Whoever follows Me will not walk in darkness, but will have the light of life'"* (John 8:12).

After reading *Star of Wonder* to your child, point out stars around you: Christmas decorations, designs on wrapping paper, and in the night sky. Tell your child that every time we see a star, we can remember the one that led the Wise Men to the Christ Child. Christ is the Star of salvation, announced by Old Testament prophets, that brought eternal light into our world. If your child is old enough, sing together an Epiphany hymn such as "As with Gladness Men of Old" or "Songs of Thankfulness and Praise."

The Editor